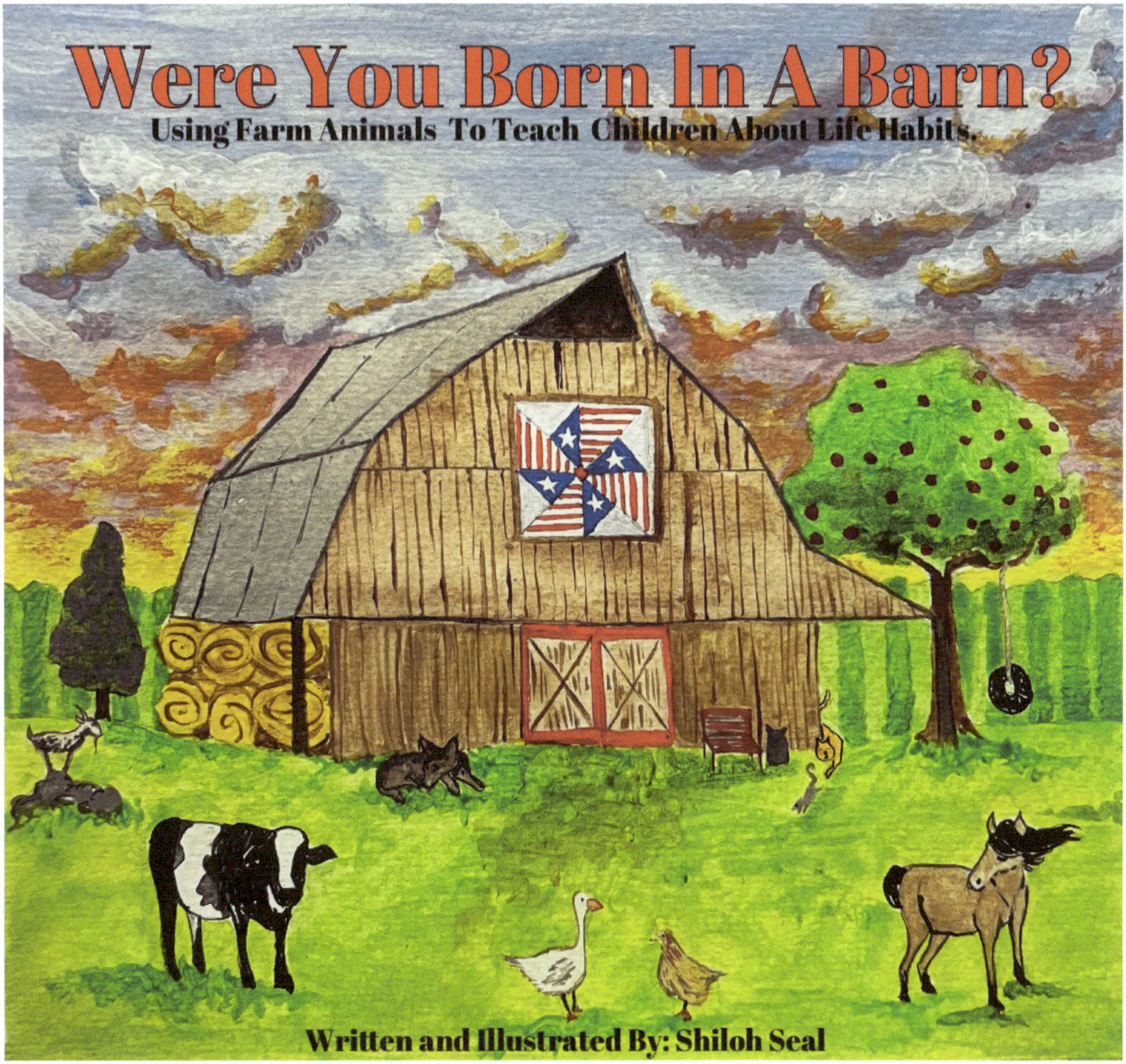

Were You Born In A Barn?

Using Farm Animals To Teach Children About Life Habits.

Written and Illustrated By: Shiloh Seal

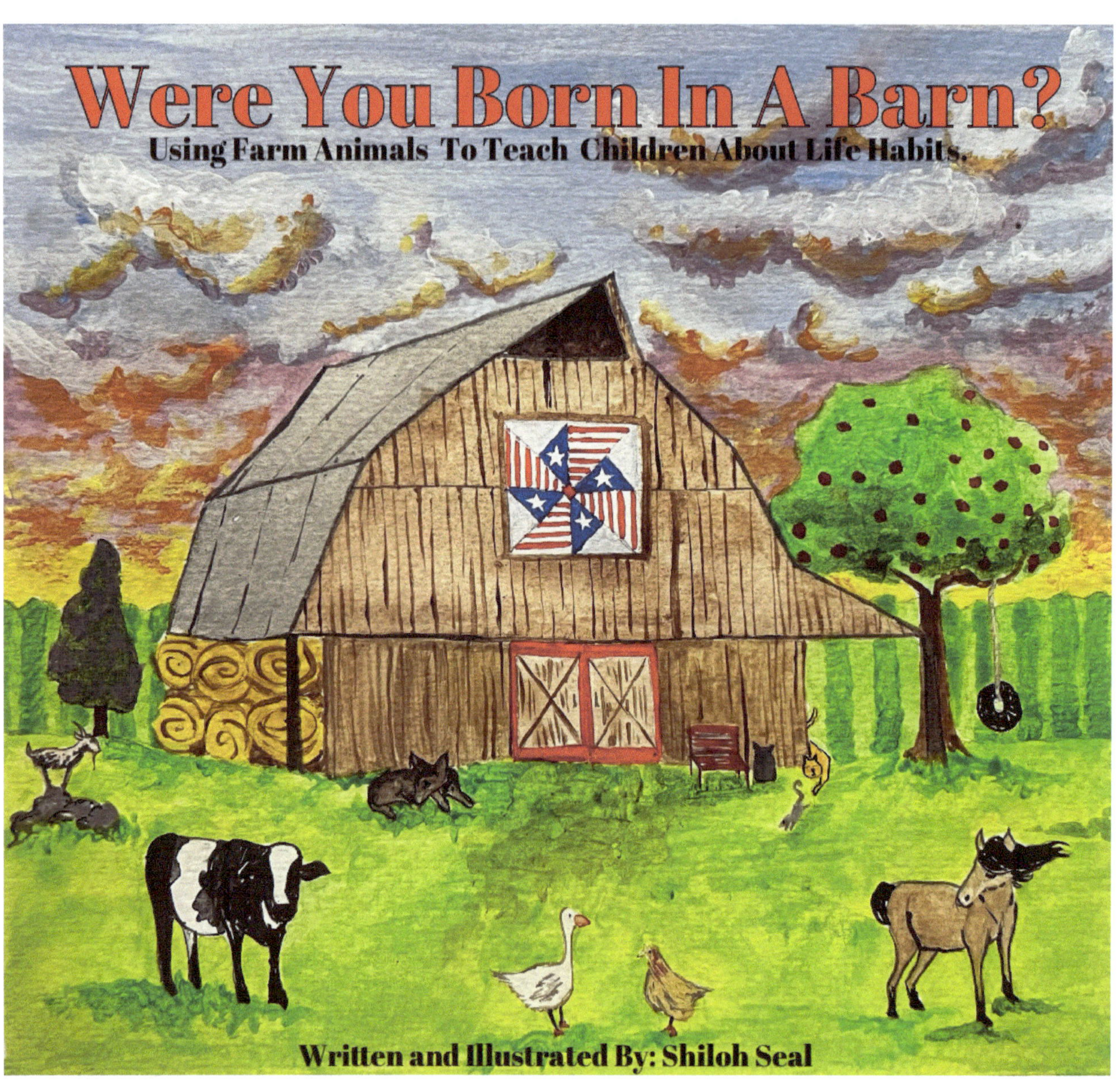

Were You Born In A Barn?
Using Farm Animals To Teach Children About Life Habits.
Written and Illustrated By: Shiloh Seal

****

Dedicated to all our children, with love. You keep life fun
and inspire creativity every day. May you always know
you were created to move mountains.

Horses sleep standing up.

We sleep lying in our cozy beds.
Were you born in a barn?

Sheep make their beds
by rustling grass or hay.

We make our beds by pulling our blankets up and laying them them neatly over our beds.
I Corintians 6:13
Were you born in a barn?

Rabbits chew on wood
to keep their
teeth healthy and strong.

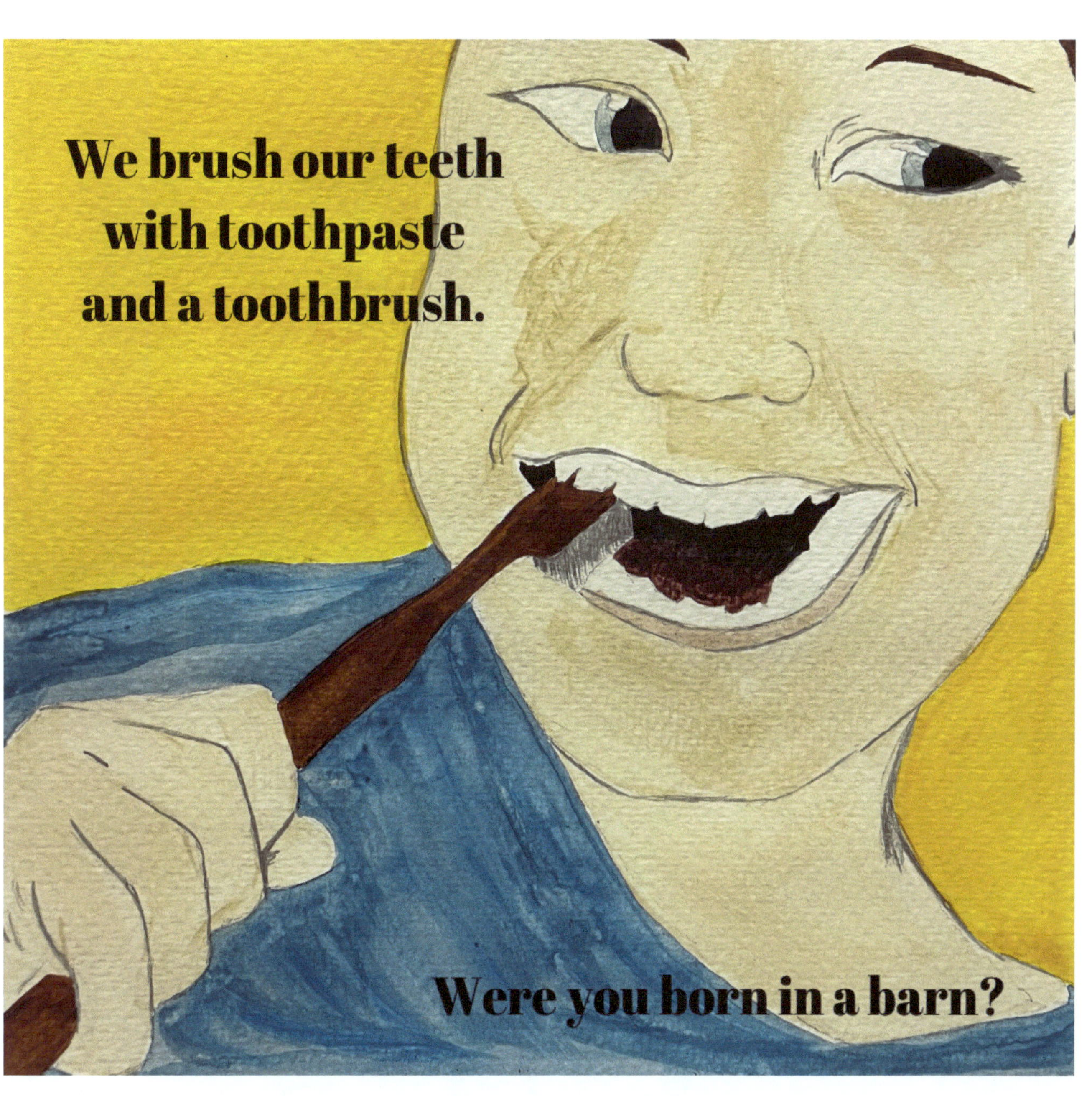

We brush our teeth
with toothpaste
and a toothbrush.
Were you born in a barn?

Cats lick their
fur to give
themselves
a bath.

We scrub our bodies in a bathtub.
Were you born in a barn?

Mice steal food from others.

We grow our food in gardens.
Were you born in a barn?

Cows stand and graze in fields to eat grass.

We sit at the table with our family.
Were you born in a barn?

Pigs leave scraps
from their meals lying all over.

We always clear our spots.
We put our dishes in the sink to get washed.
Were you born in a barn?

Geese honk loudly everywhere they go.

We use
quiet
voices
when we
are
inside.
Were you born in a barn?

Goats climb on everything.

We sit on furniture the proper way.
We never put
our feet on it.
Were you born in a barn?

Ducks splash when they play in the water.
Then they waddle away without a care.

We clean up our mess when we are done playing.
We always put our toys away.
TOYS
Were you born in a barn?

Chicken drop their
feathers all over the coop.

We put our clothes inside a hamper.
Were you born in a barn?

JOSHUA 24:15
Dogs push open doors to come inside.

We always shut doors after we open them.
Were you born in a barn?

"Honor your father and mother, that your days may be long upon the land which the Lord your God is giving you."

Exodus 20:12 NKJV

****

"Commit your works to the Lord, and your thoughts will be established."

Proverbs 16:3 NKJV

THE END

www.ingramcontent.com/pod-product-compliance
Lightning Source LLC
Chambersburg PA
CBHW042015110726
48006CB00004B/1098